PING-PONG

THE AUTHOR

PING-PONG
Reg. in U.S. Patent Office

THE GAME
ITS TACTICS AND LAWS

By CORNELIUS G. SCHAAD
Captain of the New Rochelle Independents
Member of The American Ping-Pong Association
The Metropolitan Ping-Pong Association of N.Y. and
The University Club of Mt. Vernon, N.Y.

WITH INTRODUCTORY COMMENT BY
WILLIAM T. TILDEN, 2ND
AND
FRANCIS T. HUNTER

COACHWHIP PUBLICATIONS
Greenville, Ohio

Ping-Pong, by Cornelius G. Schaad
© 2013 Coachwhip Publications
Front cover: Ping-pong paddle © Justin Skinner. Back cover: Ping-pong © DW Photos.
No claims made on public domain material.
Published 1930.

ISBN 1-61646-224-8
ISBN-13 978-1-61646-224-6

CoachwhipBooks.com

CONTENTS

Publisher's Announcement	11
Preface	13
Illustrations	15
From Introduction to First Manual	17
Introduction	19
I. Ping-Pong	23
II. General History of Ping-Pong	27
III. The American Ping-Pong Association	32
IV. The Future of the Game in America and Three Possible Champions	34
V. Ping-Pong Equipment	42
TABLE	42
THE BALL	44
NETS	44
POSTS	44
SPACE AND LIGHTING	45
VI. The Science of Play	46
HOW TO HOLD A RACKET	46
SPIN STROKE	47
GENERAL RULES FOR ALL STROKES	49
SERVICE	50
SPIN SERVICE	50
RETURN OF SERVICE	52
THE DOUBLES GAME	53
FREAK DOUBLES	55
VII. The Strokes of the Game	56
1. FOREHAND STROKES	56
2. BACKHAND STROKES	57

CONTENTS

3. CHOP-STROKES. CUT-STROKES AND TWISTS		61
4. THE SMASH		62
5. LOBBING		62

VIII. The Best Methods of Practice ... 66

IX. 'Do's and Don'ts' or Hints on Advanced Play ... 71

X. Ping-Pong for Ladies ... 75

XI. How to Organize and Run a Ping-Pong Tournament ... 76
- EQUIPMENT ... 77
- ENTRIES ... 78
- THE DRAW ... 79
- BLIND DRAW ... 80
- SEEDED DRAW ... 80
- TOURNAMENT OFFICIALS ... 82

The Laws of Ping-Pong ... 85
- A. THE PING-PONG TABLE ... 85
- B. THE PING-PONG BALL ... 86
- C. THE PING-PONG NET AND POSTS ... 86
- PING-PONG SINGLES ... 86
  1. THE SERVER AND THE RECEIVER ... 87
  2. CHOICE OF SERVICE OR COURT ... 87
  3. THE MATCH, THE GAME AND THE SCORING ... 87
  4. THE CHANCE OF ENDS ... 87
  5. THE SERVICE ... 87
  6. A GOOD SERVE: THE BOUNCE BALL SERVICE ... 87
  7. A GOOD RETURN ... 89
  8. THE SEQUENCE OF PLAY ... 89
  9. THE BALL IN PLAY ... 89
  10. A POINT ... 90
  11. A DEAD BALL ... 90
  12. A LET ... 91
  13. A FAULT ... 91
  14. A RALLY ... 91

CONTENTS 9

PING-PONG DOUBLES	91
15. PING-PONG DOUBLES	91
16. CHOICE OF SERVICE	92
17. A GOOD DOUBLES SERVE	92
18. THE SEQUENCE OF DOUBLES PLAY	92
LAWN TENNIS COURT FOR SCORING	93
AUTHORIZED EQUIPMENT	94
THE PING-PONG TABLE	94
THE PING-PONG BALL	95
THE PING-PONG NET AND POSTS	95
THE PING-PONG RACKET	95

PUBLISHERS' ANNOUNCEMENT

THE author of this book upon Ping-Pong, Mr. Schaad, modestly disclaims authority as an expert. Those, however, who have either played with Mr. Schaad or seen his play, realize that his reputation as a player (which has been obtained by his activities in this line in Manhattan and greater New York) is justified and that he speaks from experience and practice, rather than theory. He has written with love for the game and in order to stimulate the already enormous interest to greater proportions. He believes there are many players who, though they play often, have no experience in high class Ping-Pong, and that such players remain in a condition of self-satisfied contentment, entirely ignorant of their limitations. It is hoped that these pages will open the eyes of many to the real possibilities and skill in this fascinating game.

Mr. Schaad writes, 'In addition to my cordial thanks for the aid received from the leading players of America in the preparation of this book, I wish to give special acknowledgement and thanks to Messrs. Parker Brothers, of Salem, Mass., and New York who have produced the great indoor game during the long period of years since its inception, both for their assistance and for permission to use their famous title for this manual. They have cordially coöperated and collaborated with the American Ping-Pong Association and committees of prominent players for the best interests of the game.'

PREFACE

THE game of Ping-Pong as played in America to-day has passed the experimental stage and even the most skeptical admit that it is not a passing fad, but is here to stay. Since the publication of my little Manual in 1928, there have been important changes in the Laws of Ping-Pong as adopted by the American Ping-Pong Association in an effort to standardize the game in this country. These changes have been worked out and adopted after considerable experimentation by leading players throughout the nation. It is believed that the game as now played under the rules of the American Ping-Pong Association offers a standard of play that should be adopted by all clubs and individuals alike. The changes in the rules and the rapid progress of the game have made it necessary to make a new and enlarged edition of my previous book in order to bring it up to date.

Two of the most drastic changes in the rules have been the introduction of the 'bounce ball' service which does away with the confusion that formerly resulted because of the constant uncertainty as to the legality of the old 'under the waist' service and the standardization of the doubles game. In doubles play the alternative style of play is used, but service is made right to left, left to right, as in lawn tennis.

It has been very gratifying to the author to hear from players all over the country that they have found his manual practical and useful in the past.

The game has increased tremendously in popularity during the last few years. It is played by people in every walk of life. Thus we hear of it being played in schools and colleges, on

PREFACE

ocean liners, in mining camps, in Y.M.C.A.'s, in college fraternity houses, at country clubs, in private homes, and in the big athletic clubs of the country. Tournaments are being held everywhere.

It is interesting to learn that the game is popular in the movie colony at Hollywood, and we hear of such celebrities as Joan Crawford, Florence Vidor, Dorothy Mackail, Loretta Young, Alice White, Billie Dove, John Barrymore, James Cruze and others getting exercise and pleasant relaxation from this wonderful game.

The big climax of the 1930 Tournament season came in March, when an open Tournament under the auspices of The American Ping-Pong Association was held by one of its largest branches, The Metropolitan Ping-Pong Association of New York, in the Salon Moderne of the Hotel Pennsylvania in New York City. The standard of play, the many participants and the enthusiastic galleries stamped the Hotel Pennsylvania tournament as the biggest and most successful ever held.

Not only has the game increased in popularity, but the quality of play has advanced since the publication of the first edition of my manual. Many new stars have cropped up all over the country and taken the lime light away from some of the older players.

It has been the author's aim to make his book as practical as possible for both the expert and the beginner. If the first edition has proved helpful, it is hoped that this new edition will be even more so.

CORNELIUS G. SCHAAD

New Rochelle, N.Y.
1930

ILLUSTRATIONS

THE AUTHOR	*Frontispiece*
MR. WILLIAM G. TILDEN, 2ND	25
MR. FRANCIS T. HUNTER, VICE-PRESIDENT OF THE AMERICAN PING-PONG ASSOCIATION, PRESENTING CHAMPIONSHIP CUP TO MR. MARCUS SCHUSSHEIM, WINNER OF THE METROPOLITAN PING-PONG TOURNAMENT, AT THE HOTEL PENNSYLVANIA, NEW YORK, MARCH, 1930	37
LAWN TENNIS GRIP — FOREHAND	59
AUTHOR'S BACKHAND GRIP	59
FREAK GRIP — FRONT VIEW	63
FREAK GRIP — BACK VIEW	63
PENHOLDER GRIP OF MR. W. C. WELLS, JR.	67

From INTRODUCTION TO FIRST MANUAL
By William T. Tilden, 2nd

Just a word about Ping-Pong for the uninitiated. Ping-Pong is a particular form of indoor tennis. It is a game owned and developed by Parker Brothers, and its great growth has carried it into national importance. Let me state at once that Ping-Pong as a game has many of the best qualities of competitive athletics, far more than any of the smaller indoor games. The old myth that Ping-Pong hurts one's tennis is ridiculous and unfounded. There is no cause for fear on the score. All over the United States groups of Ping-Pong enthusiasts hold local championships.

The American Ping-Pong Association will aid in standardizing rules and equipment, help develop Ping-Pong clubs and encourage tournaments, even striving in the not distant future to effect International Matches. In effect this organization will strive to do for Ping-Pong what the Golf and Tennis Associations have done for their games.

No game can succeed without organization, and The American Ping-Pong Association should prove a tremendous asset to the game. Every group of Ping-Pong fans and players should welcome such a move. Join the organization and use with scrupulous care the equipment and rules adopted for play by The American Association. I am a great believer in standardized rules and equipment for any game that is played in any international, or even national sense.

This little book by Mr. Schaad is a valuable manual to

Ping-Pong for in it an expert player tells why and how he plays the game and tells it in language that a novice can understand and profit by. One finds a clear exposition of stroke technique, tactics, grips and all the essentials of play told with the enthusiasm that is necessary to success.

I have played Ping-Pong for years! It has a real fascination for me. I find it has the same for many of my friends. Jackie Coogan is a keen enthusiast, Gloria Swanson plays regularly. Manual Alonso and Vincent Richards are excellent players. One finds Ping-Pong enthusiasts in the world of art, theater, music, motion picture, medicine, law, as well as the great business world. Ping-Pong affords relaxation, exercise, and amusement in sound and sane proportions! I hope the American Ping-Pong Association succeeds in its aims and that the next few years will see the growth in the game that it deserves.

INTRODUCTION

By Francis T. Hunter

PING-PONG is one of the most popular indoor games in the world and deservedly so. Its appeal is unlimited and it is enthusiastically played by game lovers of all ages. It develops dexterity, alertness and accuracy, qualities that are essential in playing golf, tennis, and other outdoor games.

In Westchester County, where the game has met with the greatest popularity, many have devoted an entire room in their home, garage or barn to Ping-Pong. These 'Ping-Pong rooms' are the scenes of many exciting tournaments, which are run off in the same manner as a tennis tournament. Not only matches in men's and ladies' singles are held but doubles and mixed doubles are also very popular. After the final match, an exhibition is frequently given by two of the champions, and it is here that only a well-trained eye can occasionally catch a glimpse of the ball. Many ladies have become exceptionally expert players and vie with the men for first honor. Handicaps should be given beginners and inexperienced players by spotting them a point or more each game. This will not only serve to encourage the new players but also make competition more interesting.

Although quite a number of suburban dwellers have done so, it is fortunately not necessary to devote an entire room to the playing of Ping-Pong. The folding table makes it possible for this game to be enjoyed in the dining room or living room of any apartment. Most clubs, city and country, have one or more tables available for members and one new New York motion picture theater has constructed an elaborate room where patrons can play Ping-Pong while waiting for the beginning of the picture.

Ping-Pong has proven itself an incomparable game for those who seek a pleasant pastime. To those who have taken it up more seriously with the aspiration of becoming a champion, Ping-Pong is a fascinating hobby.

I believe the popularity of the game has reached a point where Ping-Pong has become a household word in the homes of most American sportspeople. Personally, I play it a great deal, particularly in winter, and in fact have a room in my home especially set aside for Ping-Pong. Many of the world's greatest tennis players, and other prominent sports stars as well, have enjoyed spirited competition on my table.

To derive the greatest benefit from Ping-Pong, I suggest that players in each community form local clubs, of good players (or those who show an indication of becoming so), with the intention of making application for branch membership in the American Ping-Pong Association. The acceptance of clubs in the association renders them eligible for representation in inter-state and national tournaments, and for the eventual international tournament which will ultimately be planned to follow in the sequence of events. The interests of the sport and its advancement are best served through this membership, and fortunately in this country Ping-Pong, through the strong position of the American Ping-Pong Association and its powerful backing, rests in good and safe hands.

Francis T. Hunter

1930.

PING-PONG

PING-PONG

CHAPTER I
PING-PONG

PING-PONG! The sound of the ball as racket meets ball is to the pongist as music is to the singer. What is the game? It is related to and somewhat similar to Lawn Tennis but played upon a table. Ping-Pong is the accepted indoor game. Because of its definitely distinguishing standard rules of play, special table markings, the absolute uniformity of its prescribed, authorized equipment and the responsible single source of its origin, Ping-Pong must not be confused with table tennis, a game of often conflicting rules, miscellaneous sources and non-standard equipment.

The game can be played to advantage on a small table in the average home as this is excellent practice for play on a club or tournament size table. In fact, the dining-room table is most frequently used, upon which the required lengthwise center line is laid out with tape or twine or chalk. Thus, healthy recreation and exercise may be obtained from the pursuit of this game and many a wet afternoon, be it summer or winter, can be made more pleasant by playing this game by people who want to vary their Bridge Playing or Novel Reading. Mr. Sidney Lenz an eminent authority on the game of Bridge is also an excellent Ping-Pong player. While men undoubtedly play a faster and more expert game than women, there are many ladies who play almost as well as men, which is another reason for the game's increasing popularity in this country — in fact, all over the world.

There are many different styles of play in Ping-Pong. There is the driving game, the chop or slice and the all-court game. Some players fare much better against certain types of game.

It must, of course, not be imagined by any prospective Ping-Ponger who should happen to read this treatise that the game can be learned solely from reading a manual. Each stroke will require constant practice before any degree of efficiency can be obtained, and each intending player will have to adapt the strokes to his own peculiarities; for what is best for one player is not necessarily the best for another. To the writer, the qualities a good player must possess to excel are good nerve, sound judgment, resolution and temper under control, ability to mix spin and pace, faultless technique, together with fair sight and sympathy between hand and eye. Of these, some are the gifts of nature and cannot be acquired; others, careful training will improve. From which it will be seen that, as in all games of skill, there are bound to be some who will far surpass others in their play and the less gifted must be content with mediocrity.

CHAPTER II
GENERAL HISTORY OF PING-PONG

THE origin of Ping-Pong came as the result of an evolution in certain miniature types of Tennis games. In the early nineties one game in particular, produced in this country but exploited principally through the London house of the makers, had, probably on account of its sale abroad, a direct suggestive influence.

This game of indoor tennis was played with small size rackets or battledores, using a firm light ball covered with a knitted web to avoid harm to furniture and other articles, with a small size net, which could be used either across a dining-room table or, if played on the floor, between the backs of chairs. Some one having association with the concern of Hamley Brothers in London, who were dealers in sporting goods and handled the above game, conceived the use or substitution of a celluloid ball. Just who this was cannot now be surely stated as there were several claimants, a Mr. James Gibb being the most frequently mentioned in this connection. This contribution coupled with a vellum battledore and a lower net, with improved table adjustments, developed into the better and prominent game, as we know it to-day. The Hamleys, quick to realize the excellent possibilities in this new development and its advantages over any indoor tennis attempts previously produced, originated the fanciful title Ping-Pong and made immediate registration in Stationers' Hall and in the Copyright Office and Patent Office in Washington. The sound made by vellum battledores when striking the ball back and forth suggested the world-famous word. Securing the association and services of the Parkers of Salem (whose London house had exploited the indoor tennis above referred to) the Hamleys together with Jaques and Son, with whom they had also made connection, devoted especial attention to the development of the game in London by tournaments at Queen's Hall on Regent Street, which attracted much attention, and which coupled with the publication of a book by Mr. Arnold Parker, widely circulated at the time, did much to bring the game into overwhelming popularity.

During the furor that followed and which reached its greatest climax in the winter, spring, and early summer of 1902, wooden, rubber and cork covered rackets, as well as the sanded and leather covered Ping-Pong rackets now so much in vogue, were substituted for the vellum battledores. The balls then not so perfectly made, as now, were developed finally into a measured and weighted product, the Match Ping-Pong Ball, one of such excellence that it has only recently been excelled by the development of the Official Ping-Pong Ball, adopted in 1929 by the American Ping-Pong Association.

Ping-Pong very quickly after its conception and the publication of the Laws of Ping-Pong, which were developed by the leading players and copyrighted in 1901 and 1902, was played vigorously all over the world. It became one of those wave crazes which know no bounds. It was perhaps over-played, too much dilated upon and understood as a craze and a reaction followed for a few years, in which period Ping-Pong was played only by those who had developed such scientific and skillful performance as to make the game not the whim of a moment, but a lasting indoor sport worthy of the capable racket or tennis player. The immense success of Ping-Pong

GENERAL HISTORY OF PING-PONG 29

bred immediately a large number of similar games of different and unstandardized manufacture and generally without a definite brand, but made by various concerns under the commercial title of table tennis. This title carried to certain groups the idea that the game should be played and scored like outdoor tennis, and tables were made by furniture manufacturers, marked off like miniature tennis courts, a plan which is not in the least suitable for the game of Ping-Pong, and which lead to the 'Love-40' game type of scoring, which is quite different from that called for by the Laws of Ping-Pong as adopted by the Ping-Pong Association.

Ping-Pong differs from Table Tennis in the arrangement of courts which are not as originally and ordinarily used in the tennis game, in certain methods of play, and in the use of the Laws of Ping-Pong as developed by the best players and approved by the Ping-Pong Association, and in the still more important fact that there is a standardized type of utensils made under the recommendations of an experienced committee of the best-known players and adopted in part or whole by the American Ping-Pong Association. The title, Table Tennis, is, generally speaking, a term used commercially, indicating a miscellaneous source of supply outside of the adopted game. The Ping-Pong Association has adopted the registered Ping-Pong and its laws because, among other advantages, it details a single source of responsibility, which confused and unstandardized sources of production cannot possess.

While Ping-Pong has been steadily played, the number of players constantly increasing, it has now reached a point of prominence, which is known as a 'Revival' in both America and Europe. Among the world's best players curiously enough, the Hungarians have developed a surprising list of champions, but America, China, England, Japan, France, Germany, Austria, Sweden, Czecho-Slovakia, Australia, and the American and English social colonies everywhere, whether in Cairo or other resorts, are now playing the game, not as a fad or craze, but as a most excellent, fashionable and popular amusement, in which great skill is being developed. Cups for championship play are frequently donated and a cup for the American Championship will doubtless soon be offered by the American Ping-Pong Association.

In America, the reorganization of the American Ping-Pong Association and its branches is bringing Ping-Pong into organized development to an unexcelled extent. The game will be popularized through the Branch Associations in all the larger towns of the country. At present the situation in England is somewhat confused owing to the fact that one of the leading associations is compelled to carry on under the generic name of Table Tennis, due to the fact that at its organization its sponsors were unable, or failed possibly because of some mismanagement, to conclude an arrangement regarding Ping-Pong with the owners. This, unfortunately, resulted in irritability and some confusion in England and has evidenced itself in many ways, particularly in the use of heterogeneous types of equipment, especially rackets, including the rather unsportsmanlike 'barn door' racket, which, in some cases, seems large enough to stone-wall nearly any type of service, and tends toward the appearance of making a childish game of what should properly be a real sport.

That the great and small delight in Ping-Pong was prominently evidenced in the rotogravures of the press when capable and big Mr. Tilden showed little Jackie Coogan the movie star, how to improve his game. Mlle. Suzanne Lenglen

GENERAL HISTORY OF PING-PONG

and Mr. Paul Feret put on an exhibition Doubles Match in the Ball Room of the Hotel Astor about the same time, with Mary Brown and Vincent Richards. Mrs. Helen Wills Moody and Miss Marjorie Morrill, tennis stars of the first magnitude, are excellent players and lovers of Ping-Pong.

The increase in the popularity of the game in this country during the past two years has been phenomenal. The game has spread from coast to coast and from border to border. It is just as popular on the Atlantic Coast as it is on the Pacific Coast, and in our Central States, particularly in such cities as Chicago and Cleveland, the country clubs have taken it up in a real competitive way.

Many people play the game for the fun they get out of it; others for the healthful recreation they derive from it, while still others take it very seriously and go in for it with the same enthusiasm as they do baseball, football, basketball, or any other major sport.

CHAPTER III

THE AMERICAN PING-PONG ASSOCIATION

THE American Ping-Pong Association, formed by a number of experienced players and authorities on the game, is the parent of all Ping-Pong associations in this country. One of the chief functions of this national organization is to organize and conduct State and National tournaments, which will eventually culminate in an international tournament. The American Ping-Pong Association also has adopted uniform laws of play, and has aided the standardization of equipment. It has also assisted in the formation of affiliated clubs throughout the country and has stimulated Ping-Pong tournaments and matches between them properly conducted under the official laws.

It is through these branch Ping-Pong clubs that the greatest opportunity for sport may be found. A club can conduct team matches and tournaments that would be impossible for individual players without organization, and have representation in the larger affairs and tournaments for State and National championship. It is my hope to see the development of the American Ping-Pong Association soon reach a point which will make it one of the largest organizations of its nature in existence.

Membership in the American Ping-Pong Association is open to all clubs of recognized standing in the country. Small groups of players may also, provided they form a definite and well-reputed organization, become members of the Association; in fact, I urge players in communities where there is no

THE AMERICAN PING-PONG ASSOCIATION 33

Ping-Pong Club to form one, even though at first small, and apply for admission to the Association. Membership in the parent body will entitle these clubs to representation in all State and National tournaments and in the International Tournament that is being planned for eventual occurrence. The tournament held by the Metropolitan Ping-Pong Association under the auspices of the American Association at the Hotel Pennsylvania in March, 1930, was the greatest Ping-Pong contest ever held, and larger and more important plans will later be developed.

Local organizations should apply to the Secretary for such information as will enable them to establish good standing and make them eligible for membership. The American Ping-Pong Association has full authority, through the copyright owners, to use the name 'Ping-Pong,' as in its own case, in connection with all branches accepted by it for membership in the organization, and its voted recommendations as to equipment are adopted and carefully produced immediately by the owners as the standard Ping-Pong equipment.

The secretary of The American Ping-Pong Association is W. Sidney Felton, Esq., whose address is No. 1 Federal St., (11th Floor) Boston, Mass.

CHAPTER IV
THE FUTURE OF THE GAME IN AMERICA AND THREE POSSIBLE CHAMPIONS

THE question arises as to the future possibilities of Ping-Pong in this country. Once merely a fad, the game has now come into its own and can be ranked with tennis and golf as one of the leading sports in American recreational life. More tournaments will be held, open, invitation, and club. Intersectional team matches are sure to be held within the next year or so, and it is highly probable that an International Tournament will be staged by the American Ping-Pong Association in connection with the coming World's Fair to be held in Chicago, or perhaps previous to that event.

But great as has been the improvement in the standard of play during the last few years, we must not lose sight of the fact that we Americans have much to learn about the game. The leading players on the Continent of Europe are superior in skill to our leading American players. This is only natural as the European countries have long played the game very intently and seriously indeed and are more advanced in the use of spin. The Hungarians especially are marvelous players.

It is the writer's opinion that our best players are to be found in and around New York City. This is due chiefly to the fact that many of the leading New York players have had their early training in the game on the other side, and are thoroughly at home with the 'bounce ball' method of serving and the various spins which are new to most American players. The writer has personally played leading players from

THE FUTURE OF THE GAME IN AMERICA 35

Cleveland and Chicago, and while the Middle Westerners can hold their own against plain hit strokes, they have trouble in returning the various spin serves and cut strokes. The writer cannot emphasize too strongly to all American players to try and use more spin in all their strokes. Spin is the basic principle of Ping-Pong and when spin is imparted to the ball, such strokes are hard to return. It may be easy to drive back a plain hit ball, but try and return a heavily spun drive with top spin and watch the result. It is only a question of time, probably within the next season, that our Middle Western friends will familiarize themselves with the use of spin in their game. Already leading players from that section of the country have had the benefit of playing against leading New Yorkers, and they in turn will coach their fellow players in the home clubs.

The writer has often been asked to name the leading players in America to-day. It is difficult to say and at most is only a matter of opinion. Every section has its local champions and we do not have the opportunity to see them all in action. But from my own observation and study of players in actual tournament play, I name Schussheim of the Boys' Club of New York, Court Gerstmann of the New York Ping-Pong Club, and Chet Wells of the University Club of Mt. Vernon, N.Y., as three of the outstanding ones among the best. Mr. Tilden and Mr. Hunter are naturally very expert and brilliant players.

California has had a State Ping-Pong Championship tournament for the past five years and the members of the movie colony at Hollywood consider it one of their favorite pastimes. But the biggest tournament ever held in this country was that played in the Salon Moderne on the Hotel Pennsylvania Roof, New York City, March 24 to March 28, 1930, under the auspices of the Metropolitan Ping-Pong Association of New York, a branch of the American Ping-Pong Association. Nine tables were in constant use with an umpire at every table, and the skill shown by the majority of the players entered showed how rapidly the game has progressed in this country. Crowds attended this tournament and the galleries were exceedingly appreciative and generous in applauding the good play of the participants.

M. Schussheim, representing the Boys' Club of New York City, won the tournament after a spectacular victory over Court Gerstmann, New York Ping-Pong Club star. Schussheim, who also won the Eastern Ping-Pong title at Brooklyn, N.Y., is probably the outstanding player in this country to-day. His machine-like perfection is almost unbelievable and yet people who think Schussheim is merely a good defensive player do not know what a marvelous player the young man really is. True, he has the best defense of any player in the country, but he has much more than that. He is forcing all the time and one has to play against him to appreciate his real skill. He has that rare ability to raise his game as occasion demands and has beaten Gerstmann in at least four tournament finals. Gerstmann, the runner-up, and former champion of Berlin, Germany, employs every stroke in the game and is easily the most brilliant and interesting player to watch we have yet seen in this country. Gerstmann never plays safe. He attacks constantly, has blinding speed, being able to drive with equal facility with either fore or back hand, has beautiful cut shots and knows how to mix spin strokes with his drives. He has beautiful form and has an easy, graceful motion that makes every stroke look simple. With the exception of

MR. FRANCIS T. HUNTER, VICE-PRESIDENT OF THE AMERICAN PING-PONG ASSOCIATION, PRESENTING CHAMPIONSHIP CUP TO MR. MARCUS SCHUSSHEIM, WINNER OF THE METROPOLITAN PING-PONG TOURNAMENT, AT THE HOTEL PENNSYLVANIA, NEW YORK, MARCH, 1930

THE FUTURE OF THE GAME IN AMERICA 39

Schussheim, most other Americans have been easy for Gerstmann. He has defeated among others in exhibition matches Cedric Major, who has been a leading player in the New York district for many years.

F. George of the Art Guild, a veteran at the game who beats many of the younger stars because of his scientific game, also took part in the tournament. His strategy often counteracts the disadvantage against the natural quickness of eye and hand that the youngsters have. Other good players in the tournament were W. C. Wells, Jr., of Mt. Vernon, N.Y., Walter Gray, a former champion of Scotland, but now residing in Jersey City, N.J., leading exponents of the so-called Pen-holder Grip, and Kitara Tamada, Japanese star.

Francis T. Hunter, Vice President of The American Ping-Pong Association, one of the highest ranking tennis players in this country, was the official referee of the tournament, umpired the final match and presented the silver cup to the winner, M. Schussheim. About 340 players took part in this particular tournament.

The progress of the tournament was reported by many of the New York newspapers and action pictures were shown all over the country in the newsreels.

One of the events of the 1929 season was the visit of Raymond Verger, champion of France, to New York City. The most exciting Ping-Pong match the writer has ever seen was that between Verger and Gerstmann in the final of an invitation tournament held in Brooklyn, N.Y. The match went the full five games with Verger just nosing out Gerstmann. This match was so spectacular and colorful that all who witnessed it agreed that Ping-Pong at its best was as dramatic and exciting as any of our major sports.

Newspaper articles from such widely separated states as Maine, Virginia, West Virginia, Maryland, Minnesota, Illinois, Texas, Tennessee, Alabama, California, Colorado, Oregon, Washington and Ohio, tell us about tournaments and local champions. Thus we learn that at Santa Barbara, Cal., Charles Kelly and Norman Notley, two English singers engaged in a match with Charles Homer Paine and Leroy Linnard.

Paine was the Ping-Pong champion of the Royal College of Art in London during his school days, and Kelly and Notley have played in numerous English tournaments where they carried off many honors.

The Filmograph (Los Angeles) tells us that Mervyn LeRoy, first National Director won the championship of Malibu Beach. The latter place is one of California's beautiful beach colonies reserved exclusively for prominent film people.

The Minneapolis (Minn.) Evening Tribune of April 23, 1930, records the holding of an All-University tournament at the University of Minnesota, which is to be an annual affair. The champion was Merle Parent of Sioux City, Iowa. The runner-up was Arnold McCartney, also of Sioux City.

The Wilmette (Ill.) Life of March 21, 1930, tells of a contest for the championship of the Shawnee Club and of plans being made for international matches to be held in connection with the coming World's Fair of 1933, in Chicago.

The Philadelphia Public Ledger of March 25, 1930, records the fact that Maxwell Rudolph won the city championship of Philadelphia from a large field of more than 125.

The Middletown (N.Y.) Herald and Times of February 19, 1930, reports that Dr. Sam W. Mills, called the Tilden of Ping-

THE FUTURE OF THE GAME IN AMERICA 41

Pong, has been beating all the experts of Orange County, N.Y., in love sets.

The Syracuse (N.Y.) American of March 9, 1930, tells of Mrs. Elwyn Lawrence Smith winning a Ladies' Tournament held at the Sedgwick Farm Club with 222 ladies participating.

City championship tournaments have been held in New York, Philadelphia, Chicago, Cleveland and Spokane, Washington. In 1929 Cornell University held a tournament with 100 entrants. Keating C. Rice, a Freshman, was the winner, and the last man young Rice played was the man who had beaten the champion of Canada. Ping-Pong is very popular at Akron (O.) University, where members of Phi Delta Theta Fraternity have been experimenting with the game. Next year plans are on foot for a tournament with a series of interfraternity and sorority marches.

In the early part of 1930 the first Chicago District Championship Tournament was played at the Highland Park Club. There were 84 entrants with seven tables, the entire tournament being played by the process of elimination in one night. Mr. Ray Leininger came off champion with Coleman Clark of the Interfraternity Club of Chicago, runner-up. Mr. Clark, however, won the Interfraternity Handicap Championship from scratch, defeating Mr. Leininger in the finals.

All of which proves that Ping-Pong has had a healthy growth in the year 1930.

CHAPTER V

PING–PONG EQUIPMENT

STANDARDIZATION and uniformity of equipment are essential in Ping-Pong if the greatest pleasure and the keenest competition are to be enjoyed in playing this fascinating game. To insure these necessary standards of uniformity long experience has prompted the American Ping-Pong Association to adopt as official, tables, rackets, balls, nets and posts authorized to bear the mark 'Ping-Pong.'

Table.

The standard Ping-Pong table adopted for tournament play is of the folding design of ply or solid wood of sufficient thickness to guarantee the proper speed and uniform bounce of ball. Its top playing surface is rectangular, smooth, and level, nine feet long and five feet wide, painted a dull dark green with a three-quarters inch white painted line upon its outside edges and lengthwise down its center, and when erected the playing service is thirty inches above the floor. For non-tournament or informal play, a smaller table eight feet by four feet, marked in the same manner as the larger table, may be used, and most frequently dining-room tables are pressed into service. When the dining table is used, the center line may be laid out with tape, twine, or ordinary white chalk. A beautiful mahogany Ping-Pong table in dull finish with the usual white marking is now obtainable.

In Ping-Pong as in all other games played with rackets, individual theories are frequently advanced as to the details

PING-PONG EQUIPMENT

of the racket. The American Ping-Pong Association, after study by committees and the most expert individual players, has adopted as official a Ping-Pong racket with a blade six and a half inches long by five and a quarter inches wide with a beveled handle five inches in length. This racket naturally has superseded all the older type shapes and sizes allowing as it does the enjoyment of the keenest sport and the most skillful play. This recommendation, as is the case with all voted recommendations of The American Ping-Pong Association as to approved equipment, was immediately put into physical effect by the manufacturers. It is instructive to note that Schussheim at the New York Metropolitan Ping-Pong Tournament won the championship with the Official Ping-Pong sanded racket, which was, of course, of the above dimensions. There has been a mistaken idea among some of the younger players that a large racket with greater hitting surface allows the player to maintain a full cross-blade contact with the ball in executing spin strokes. Actual demonstration, however, has proved repeatedly that the moment of impact of racket and ball is so nearly instantaneous, that the actual surface contact between them is but a fraction of the face. There is really nothing to be said for the big blade except that it offers a factor of safety to the inexperienced player that is spurned by the true expert. Once in a while old style large rackets with a blade perhaps six and a half inches wide, seven inches long, and a handle of four and a half inches in length is seen in play. They are of the Hungarian type and are humorously referred to as 'barndoors' or 'pancakes.'

Every one has his preference when it comes to the character of the blade surface. Official Ping-Pong rackets are made with sanded, cork, leather, suede, rubber and plain wooden surfaces. Each blade surface has a different effect on the ball, and the player should choose the surface of racket that suits his personal style of play. Many experts prefer Ping-Pong rackets with either sanded or rubber blades, the former being more widely used throughout the country than any other.

The Ball.

The ball naturally plays a most important part in Ping-Pong. The selection and adoption of a Ping-Pong ball for tournament play has been the object of deep attention, study and experiment. A special ball accurately measured as to weight, dimension, strength, and resiliency has resulted and is the finest and most accurate product in a Ping-Pong ball, which has ever been produced. This is the ball adopted for tournament use. This is the Official Association ball. My second choice is the Match Ping-Pong ball, slightly lighter, but immensely popular and of admirable playing qualities.

Nets.

The authorized Official Ping-Pong net is dark green in color, bound with white, of suitable length to fit almost any table. The Official Tournament net is 66 inches long, thus providing for the established three inch 'over hang' beyond the table sides, required by 'The Laws.'

Posts.

While the Ping-Pong metal extension posts have been adopted for official tournament play because of their simplicity and ease of adjustment, other styles of authorized Ping-Pong metal and wooden posts suitable for all conditions met with are excellent and easily obtainable.

Space and Lighting.

In arranging the position of a table for a good Ping-Pong match, it is well to remember that the space required should be sufficient to allow, if possible, eight feet between the ends and three feet between the sides of the table and the walls of the room. When more than one table is to be used at a time, eight feet between their ends and five feet between their sides should be provided for.

Lighting is important too, for there must be adequate vision with no shadows. From long experience, I recommend a single light of say 100 watts, with frosted bulb, and twelve-inch cone shade, suspended about four feet above the center of the table. If this arrangement is not possible, see to it that the table is placed as advantageously as possible in relation to the lights available.

CHAPTER VI
SCIENCE OF PLAY

THE most important single factor in Ping-Pong is control, and the player who has the greatest control will win in the long run, provided always that he has finishing shots with which to end a rally. By control is meant the ability to hit the ball over the net and keep it within bounds, at the same time keeping the bounce of the ball low so that one's opponent will not have a chance to make a killing return.

There are among the expert players several who have developed their control to the highest possible degree and are able to return safely practically every shot. They win their matches largely on their opponents' errors, but when they meet a player who not only has good control, but who is strongly equipped with finishing drives, they are invariably beaten.

How to Hold a Racket.

The way in which the racket should be held in the hand depends entirely on the individual taste of the player, for there are numerous ways of holding it, and there are almost as many variations of the two commonest grips that I shall describe as there are players in the game.

Many leading players, both here and abroad, find what is called the Penholder Grip the most satisfactory. In holding the racket with this grip, the hitting surface, or face, is held between the thumb and forefinger, and in order to give power to the stroke made with this grip, the other fingers are placed

SCIENCE OF PLAY

behind the face of the racket. This, it will be noted, gives the necessary support. The players who use this grip claim that since they can use the same face of the racket for all strokes, both forehand and backhand, they have a great advantage over players who must turn their hand to make a backhand stroke.

The writer personally uses the lawn tennis grip and strokes from both forehand and backhand. Of course there are many variations of this grip, some players holding two fingers of the playing hand on the face of the racket.

After all is said and done, a player should use the grip that suits him the best, and with which he can hit the ball most effectively.

SPIN STROKE

As the flat drive, that is a straight low drive over the net, is the fundamental stroke in lawn tennis, so the spin stroke is the fundamental one in Ping-Pong. Against expert players using spin strokes, a simple drive without spin is useless.

To put spin on a Ping-Pong ball the player must draw the face of the racket across the ball practically at right angles to the path of the ball. There is little if any forward motion of the racket used in making this stroke, it is almost a vertical one. Naturally the harder the player hits the ball, the more forward motion there will be to the racket. But even in a hard shot the forward motion is extremely limited.

As a player becomes more skilled in the use of spin, he may take more liberties with the above rule, but for beginners at Ping-Pong, particularly those who take up the game after having played other games in which rackets are used, I advise constant practice in hitting the ball with practically a straight up and down stroke, which is very nearly the correct one.

One of the shots that a good player waits for in a match is a high bounding one that he may kill for a sure point. Therefore it is absolutely essential to keep the ball from bounding high on a return and it is the purpose of spin strokes to keep the ball low. Many good players, of whom Mr. Schussheim is one, put backspin on every shot they make in order to accomplish this. If this stroke is played correctly, the opposing player will have trouble in finding an opening to make a winning shot.

Another great advantage of a low ball is that an opponent will have great difficulty in returning it with speed and a player whose whole game is built upon his ability to make fast drives will be seriously handicapped.

In addition to the backspin shot, the pick-up, or half volley is used in Ping-Pong, not as an offensive stroke, but merely as a means of keeping the ball in play. Be sure when using this stroke against top spin that the upper edge of the racket face is tipped *toward* the net, and when using the half volley against under spin that the top edge is tilted *away* from the net. Of course against a plain drive, the racket should be held in a vertical position.

As has been said before, forcing shots must be added to steadiness in order to have a well-rounded game. The ability to keep the ball in play with lowback spun shots, and then to finish a rally with a hard long low-bounding top spun drive or a smashing kill, is invaluable to a good player.

A player must combine absolutely accurate control with a few strong point-winning shots in order to reach the top flight of expert players.

SCIENCE OF PLAY

GENERAL RULES FOR ALL STROKES

Do not fight the ball. Always go at the ball and never back away from it; all power will be taken from the blow if your weight is moving from the ball instead of toward it. A constant error of beginners is to move up too close to the ball as it approaches and then to step back as they strike. No habit could be worse than this.

Another mistake beginners often make is the desire to hit every ball hard. That is a development of skill that should come after the player has reached the expert class. Speed should never come before accuracy and it is essential first to learn steadiness so that the stroke is seldom missed, before any attempt is made to add speed to the shot.

It is far better to make a slow stroke successfully than to wildly bang the ball about the table and miss a large proportion of the returns by driving into the net or off the table.

Fast shots and kills do thrill galleries, but it is not the winning style of play even for expert players who more often fall before the steady, safe men who get everything back over the net and do not try to smash the ball every time they hit it. Let the other fellow make the errors in his efforts to show off; if you will keep the ball in play, you will be most likely to win the match in the end. Nine times out of ten the steady man beats the erratic man.

The lob or tossing the ball high may also be resorted to in returning a fast serve, but a lob unless far back on the opponent's side invariably bounds high and means a kill.

The same strategy is used in Ping-Pong as in lawn tennis. Keep your eye on the ball. Never give your opponent the shot he likes best. Keep him off balance. Play to his weakness, but not too much. By constantly playing to his weakness you only strengthen that department of his game. Mix spin and change of pace; jockey your opponent out of position. One of the best point getters is to force your opponent to back away from the table and when you get him off to one side, send the ball fast to the opposite corner. Thus you often get him out of position and he will not get over to the other side in time to make a good return. Outguess and outgeneral your opponent if you can and remember always — a good service is valuable, but not by any means the whole game. Do not rely solely on a fast service, but develop a good all-round game.

Service.

In Ping-Pong the service can be used as a powerful offensive weapon and should be used as such. Great care must be taken to serve well to prevent a short high-bounding serve, for if this happens the server instead of being on the offensive will immediately find himself on the defensive, and his service will have been of no tactical value whatsoever.

Spin Service.

As in the drive, spin is necessary in the serve if a player wants to force the play. A plain hit serve, as described above, will put the ball safely into play, but the serve should be used to win points, or failing that, to put one's opponent on the defensive.

The type of spin used in service depends on the grip that is employed. A good way to develop a spin service is to draw the racket across the ball and back. The wrist movement giving it excessive spin.

In the diagram (see page 51) S represents the point where the server hits the ball; X is the point where the ball bounces on the server's court and Y is the point where it finally lands.

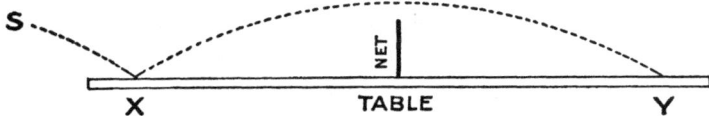

It is essential in a good serve to keep the ball well back in an opponent's court and to keep it from rising slowly or too high on its bounce. If, when the serve is made, the point where the ball touches the server's court is near the net, the ball may not clear the net, or if it clears the net, it may be over the end of the table, depending on the height of the ball when hit by the racket, point S. If, on the other hand, the ball hits the server's court near the end of the table and the start of the serve is high, the ball will, when it strikes the other court, rise to dangerous heights. Speed in this serve will not keep the ball low, but will merely add to the height of the bounce.

From this, it will be seen that the point where the server's racket first hits the ball must be low, and that the point where the ball hits the server's side of the table must be near the server's end. If these two rules are followed, one may get a low hard serve, well back in the court.

In the recent tournament held at the Pennsylvania Roof in N.Y.C., members of the Hakoah A.C. used this type of spin service at its best and in many of their matches would get as many as 10 points per game on errors off service alone. Which proves that one must not only develop a good service, but must develop a good defense as well against all types of service. This can only be acquired by constant practice against all types of service. Participation in tournaments is, of course, the best way to get the necessary experience in returning the various kinds of service.

Many players, practice as they will, never acquire a really effective spin service. Either their wrists are not flexible enough or they lack something necessary. Such players simply have services that put the ball in play and give them little or no advantage over the receiver. The only advice I can give such players is to practice and practice and practice and to watch the players with good services. Practice and patience will eventually be rewarded.

RETURN OF SERVICE

Serving, however, is only half of the game. One must know how to return any service that may be delivered. In the study of the serve, it was seen that spin is necessary for a good serve, so then it follows a player must be ready to return a spin service. A common way used by good players is to drive the serve back with top spin. This requires a good deal of practice, but will be found to be a very satisfactory method when once learned. Of course if the server should be so foolish as to serve a high bounding slow serve, one should immediately slam it back for a sure point. However, this rarely happens when playing with experts and should not be counted on as a method of returning a serve.

The great majority of players, however, will find that the defensive half volley, or pick-up shot is the most satisfactory way of returning a heavily spun service. As has been said before, this gives the receiver no particular chance of winning the point with this stroke, but is merely a safe way of keeping the ball in play provided always that the return is kept low.

When given the chance by an error of your opponents to

SCIENCE OF PLAY 53

kill a high bounding ball, by all means take it. The simplest way to kill a ball is by a straight downward stroke of the racket, and as the racket hits the ball, turn the wrist slightly to impart the spin. If this is done correctly, the ball can only be returned by phenomenal 'get' of the other player.

Some players prefer taking a fast service from well behind the table so as to take it on the bounce and not on the half-volley, or better still to chop it back. For some men, services quite impossible to take on the half-volley or pickup become comparatively easy when taken by an active player standing well back. On the other hand, some players can return the fastest serves on the half-volley and their returns usually go across the net low and fast. It is really a matter of style and personal preference.

In serving bear in mind that placing is very important. Do not forget that one must use his head as well as his wrist in the development of a good bounce ball service. Look in one direction and serve in another. Change pace. Shift your position at the table and mix speed and spin. Keep your opponent guessing as much as possible.

THE DOUBLES GAME

The doubles game in Ping-Pong is not as universally played as singles. Just why is difficult to explain. Some players claim a 9 × 5 table is too small for doubles play and that because of the limited space the partners interfere with each other. But that is what makes doubles play so fascinating. The idea is to keep out of each other's way. Team work is everything in doubles. The writer is an ardent advocate of doubles play and in a team match by all means include both singles and doubles.

The game as played in America is very much the same as in

lawn tennis except that the players must hit the ball alternately. The service is made diagonally right to left (minor court), left to right (minor court) and so on until all have served and then the process is repeated. It is a game for four people who play as partners or in pairs. The novice will find it difficult to keep out of his partner's way, but this creates no little fun and with practice the partners will seldom clash.

The tactics of doubles play are similar to lawn tennis doubles play except that no volleying is allowed. The writer has found that the ideal doubles combination is made up of a steady, machine-like player teamed up with a brilliant driver. The steady man on his returns can be counted on to keep the ball low and in play until the brilliant driver has a chance on his turn to play, to smash a fairly high return or shoot a drive through a hole in the armour of the opposing team to end the rally with an unreturnable finishing shot.

Doubles play is particularly appropriate at parties where only one table is available, players often prefer to double up and don't forget that mixed doubles — that is, a lady and gentleman on one side against a lady and gentleman on the other — provide not only plenty of action, but often much amusement. By all means encourage doubles play and if you have not tried mixed doubles, you have missed a real treat and I advise all to try it.

The writer is of the opinion that much genuine pleasure can be derived where the partners may only hit the ball alternately as described above. Such a game is good fun, calling as it does for highly developed team and foot work. It also does away with the so-called one-man doubles game. The rules adopted by the American Ping-Pong Association stipulate this style of doubles play.

Freak Doubles.

An interesting and amusing type of doubles can be played at social gatherings by allowing each pair to use only one racket between them. When one partner has made a return he immediately places the racket on the table and his partner makes the next return with the same racket. The opposing pair do the same with their racket. It can readily be seen that one cannot always pick the racket up in time. This, of course, is only a freak doubles game and is only done for the amusement it affords.

CHAPTER VII

THE STROKES OF THE GAME

1. Forehand Strokes.

Probably the most important stroke in lawn tennis is the forehand. A forehand stroke is one that is made with the ball on the same side of the body as the playing-arm — that is, on the right side for a right-handed player. This is the most natural and easy way to hit the ball, so most players use forehand strokes by preference whenever possible.

In Ping-Pong, however, the majority of players seem to be stronger on the backhand and this is mainly due to the restricted area of the playing surface. And indeed, many experts take all strokes on their backhand. On the other hand, many experts who favor a driving game take every shot they can on the forehand and on orthodox backhand returns, work around the ball so they can hit it with the forehand.

For such players, not only are forehand strokes the most important, but also the most numerous during the play, comprising more than half of the entire game. Now a forehand stroke is one made after the ball has bounded from the table, this term being used in contradistinction to volleys which are strokes made before the ball has touched the table, or 'on the fly.' Volleying or hitting the ball on the fly is not allowed in Ping-Pong.

Timing is most important in both forehand and backhand strokes. Boys who have played other ball games, particularly baseball, handball, and other games where a bounding ball is used, learn Ping-Pong much quicker, because the eye has been trained through these sports.

THE STROKES OF THE GAME

Whether from Ping-Pong itself or from some other ball game, the eye gradually becomes accustomed to the calculation that is necessary, and a fairly close guess can soon be made as to where the ball will rise to be hit and, while spin may bother the novice, the expert is able to tell the direction the ball will bound even when spin is put on the ball.

Frequently the forehand drive is called a 'loft.' This is a misnomer as there is no such stroke in the game. What they mean is a 'Lawford' named after one of the early English tennis experts. The stroke is made with a glancing blow of the racket, and this brushing motion makes the ball twist on its own axis and gives it much the same effect as the 'drop-curve' ball of a baseball pitcher, only in Ping-Pong it is called topspin. Another name for the stroke is the 'lift-stroke.' It is from the lifting motion of the racket and the dropping effect on the ball that the characteristic names of the stroke are derived. The stroke itself can be made with a short swing as there is no real follow through in Ping-Pong as in lawn tennis.

It is very important that when the racket meets the ball, it should be moving as nearly as possible in the direct line that the ball is to take. The only variation from this should be the slight upward lifting tendency of the racket that is necessary to give the topspin.

It is good practice for a beginner to stand before a mirror and go through the motions of this stroke.

2. Backhand Strokes.

All backhand strokes in Ping-Pong are distinguished from forehand strokes in that they are made with the ball on the opposite side of the body from the playing-arm. For a right-hand player, they are strokes made when the ball is played on the left side of the body.

Practically the same rules govern the playing of this stroke as already explained for the forehand. As in the forehand stroke, there are the same options regarding the best way of hitting the ball and the exact amount of twist to put on it. One can play the ball nearly straight with little or no twist or he can put topspin on the ball and give it the same dropping tendency already recommended for the forehand stroke, or he can use a chop stroke that will make the ball spin backwards in its flight. The same motions and the same style of hitting the ball are good for both the straight-hit and the topspinning ball, the chief differences being in the upward movement of the racket as it meets the ball and the finish of the stroke.

Perfect timing is essential for making a fast stroke, for it makes the racket meet the ball when carrying the maximum amount of momentum. At first most beginners time their strokes badly and even a full swing produces little speed.

Just as the ball comes in contact with the racket, the racket should be drawn slightly upward, so that it is met with a glancing blow, and kept in contact as long as possible with the ball; it should pass over it in the swing and be turned before it leaves till the upper part of the frame is forward of the lower part.

This brushing upward motion twists the ball, makes it spin on its own axis and gives it the rotation that is so effective in making it drop quickly after crossing the net. The dropping curve permits the player to hit the ball much harder and still keep it on the table. The principal features of the forehand play also apply to backhand strokes.

LAWN TENNIS GRIP — FOREHAND

AUTHOR'S BACKHAND GRIP

THE STROKES OF THE GAME

3. Chop-Strokes. Cut-Strokes and Twists.

Nearly every ball that is hit in Ping-Pong twists more or less in its own center. The ball itself is so light that it is almost impossible for the racket to hit it so directly in the line of its flight that some slight side motion will not cause it to revolve or spin around as it goes.

But this spinning is a distinct advantage, so even if you could prevent it, it would be unwise to do so. The spinning motion helps to overcome the resistance of the air.

There are in Ping-Pong many strokes that are known as cut-strokes, slice-strokes or chop-strokes. The predominating feature of all these is the under-twist on the ball that is imparted, for a cut-stroke or chop-stroke always makes the ball spin backward in a direction opposite to that used in the drop-stroke.

All of these strokes are made by striking the ball with a glancing blow, the bottom edge of the racket being forward and the face touching more of the under side of the ball than the top. In order to prevent such a blow underneath from lifting the ball up too high, the swing must be made with a downward angle.

The swing is much shorter than in the drives and is much the same as chopping with an axe. The same strokes can be played on the backhand side with much the same effect.

The greatest difficulty the player has to overcome in using the chop-stroke is its tendency to drive the ball off the table. In order to prevent this, the stroke must be played slower and with less power so it will not go too far, and this necessity robs the stroke of the speed the drive possesses.

However, with practice, great accuracy can be acquired and, as a rule, good chop-stroke players have a closer control of their slow returns than do drop-stroke players of their faster shots.

4. The Smash.

A high bounding ball near the net should as a rule be smashed as this is primarily a killing stroke. It is intended to end the rally every time and the player calculates as a rule, that he will be able to kill the ball with that stroke. He does not expect another return and the smash to kill is therefore played with great abandon. A smash once started should never be checked as the play will be ruined if any effort is made to moderate its power. He who hesitates is lost. A smash depends almost entirely on speed for its success, and it is generally not necessary to place the ball although placing of course helps. Some players can smash high bounding balls from any place on the table, but even experts often smash high bounding balls near their end of the table off the table or into the net. It is better to smash only such balls that are close to the net. This shot is of course one of the most spectacular in Ping-Pong.

5. Lobbing.

Lobbing is not as important in Ping-Pong as it is in lawn tennis chiefly because of the smaller area of playing space. The very foundation of a good defense in tennis lies in the lob. With a good lob, any player, be he beginner or expert, should be able to defend his position when pressed the hardest and from any part of the back of the court, a deep lob is almost invariably a safe answer to the hardest attack. In Ping-Pong, however, lobs are rarely used by expert players. A lob is used only when the player is so pressed that he cannot make any

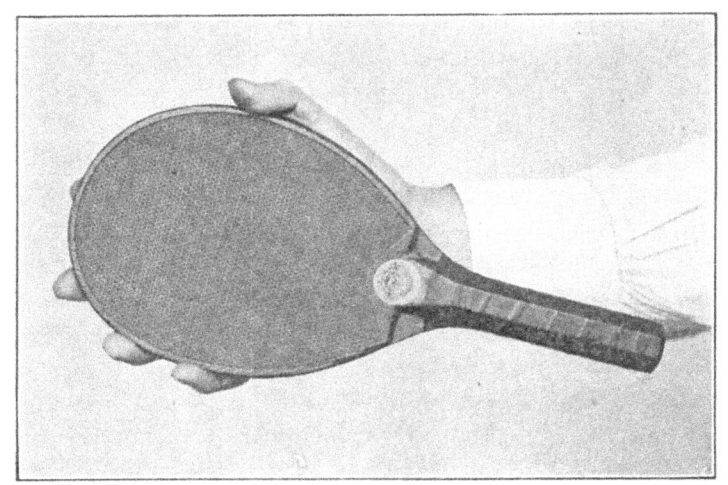

FREAK GRIP — FRONT VIEW

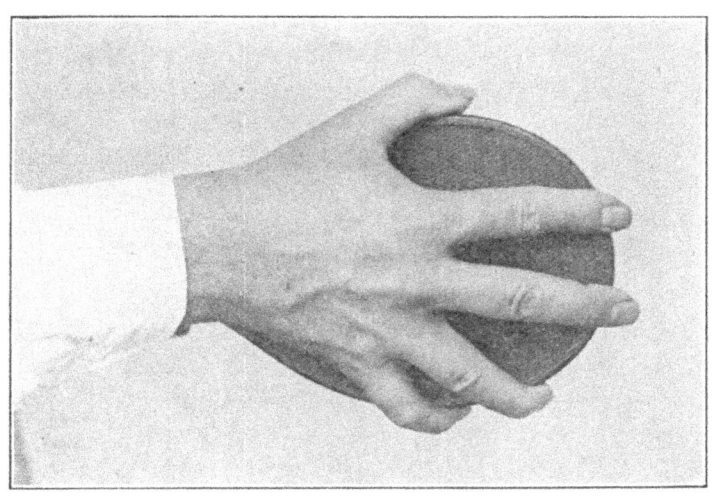

FREAK GRIP — BACK VIEW

other return or possibly he sends up an occasional lob or floater to throw an opponent off stroke. Most players think all lobs set-ups for smashes and in their overconfidence, often smash at them wildly for errors. Many good players use the lob to break up speed and sometimes purposely send up a lob for luck in an effort to bring back a high return that can be killed. Receivers, however, can cut such lobs back which should keep the ball low. It simply matches science with science.

But the stroke must be deep to be of any value at all. Nothing is more suicidal than a short lob; it is as discouraging as a fault in the service at a critical juncture and generally just as costly.

CHAPTER VIII
THE BEST METHODS OF PRACTICE

No matter how much the beginner may study the best books of the game of Ping-Pong, nothing will teach him to play, but actual practice with a racket and ball. If he has the advantage of a good coach, that is the best of all methods, for then he will have an expert or teacher close by to point out his errors as he makes them. It is very difficult to see your own faults and correct them.

The man who plays best will generally be the man who plays most providing of course he has some natural aptitude for the game. To hit the ball ten times helps a lot, a hundred still more, but a thousand strokes will generally be necessary before the novice has learned to calculate the flight and bound of the ball, and to succeed in getting the center of his racket into contact with the ball.

While it is never too late to begin to learn Ping-Pong, there is no doubt that the boy or girl who starts young will have a great advantage over the man or woman who takes up the game in middle life.

If no opponent is available, stand before a mirror and practice the various strokes of the game. You need no opponent to practice serving.

In actual practice, concentrate on the strokes you seem weakest in. It is better not to keep any score in such practice or even to play a game at all. Practice matches give less practice because each player tries to drive the ball away from the other and so you cut down the number of actual strokes that are made. It is better practice to try to play the ball

PENHOLDER GRIP OF MR. W. C. WELLS, JR.

THE BEST METHODS OF PRACTICE

each time directly toward the man on the other side, for this will increase the number of actual strokes that each has the opportunity to make in the same length of time.

In general practice play, when not in an actual match, do not hit the ball aimlessly. Indifference in practice soon breaks down a good game and often leads to indifference in match play. Even against a weaker adversary, try for each point or stop playing. If it is easy to beat the other man and you are likely to become careless, give him a handicap and even matters up in that way so you will always have to try to play your best.

By all means vary the opponents you play against. Playing always against the same men and same styles will never develop new strokes and will prevent your progress. Whenever possible get an adversary who is a little better than you are, not enough to beat you easily, but just a little better so you will be constantly trying to improve to catch up with his skill. To summarize:

Here are some good rules to follow:

1. Don't think of the score too much when you are practicing; think of your strokes and whether they are well made or not.

2. Don't be discouraged because you fail to improve every time you play; follow your progress week by week, or season by season.

3. Don't practice indifferently against poorer players; if you lose interest, stop entirely.

4. Whenever you can, get antagonists who are a little better than you are; this will pull along your game.

5. Don't practice your best strokes; they are already good, so favor your weaker point.

6. Don't fight the ball back over the net to get rid of it; have a definite objective for every stroke you make and try to place the ball where you planned.

7. When practicing strokes without a score, don't try to knock the ball out of the other man's reach; if you drive it straight at him you will both get more practice.

CHAPTER IX
'DO'S AND DON'TS' OR HINTS ON ADVANCED PLAY

Mr. Milton Work, the eminent Bridge authority, in one of his talks over the radio said you can always tell an expert Bridge Player by watching him before he makes a lead. If he pauses before playing, he is probably sizing up the situation and planning his attack or defense. The expert always plans his play. Thus it is with the Ping-Pong expert.

First of all size up your opponent. Is he temperamental? What strokes does he like to play? Has he a real weakness? Your method of attack or campaign may be planned before a match or it may be planned during play. Circumstances may make you switch from one plan to another. The game is lightning fast, therefore, an expert must think fast. Like an expert chess or checker player, a good pongist plays with his head as well as his hands. He gets mental and physical exercise. The following points may help:

1. Do not commence the game by serving too fast or driving too hard. Wait until you have become acclimated and gradually increase the pace of your service and strokes until your normal form is reached.

2. At the moment of striking the ball, whenever possible, give an upward twist to the wrist. This adds pace, makes the ball go nearer the top of the net and come quicker from the table; also if the ball strikes the top of the net this twist will, in many cases, cause it to roll over. Players who are expert in the use of spin get many net or cord shots.

3. Do not Lawford or slam at every ball. Very few players can Lawford a ball with a low bound and keep it on the table.

4. When your opponent gives you a ball which it is possible to kill, never hesitate from careful motives, but try to win the point outright. Do not be over cautious. Be aggressive and take chances. Carry the attack to your opponent as much as possible.

5. In placing the ball always send it to the spot most inconvenient to your opponent. The most inconvenient spot as a rule is that part of the court he least expects the ball to be returned to. Thus a ball straight at him down the table is very often a more telling stroke than one down one of the side lines. Also it is frequently more effective to place the ball to that part of the table his racket has just left rather than to the side it is being moved towards.

6. Try and outguess your opponent and anticipate the direction of his returns. When you hit with your backhand, your average opponent usually moves over to his left anticipating a ball on his backhand. Fool him by driving with your backhand occasionally down his forehand side line.

7. Do not lob against an opponent who can drive hard from the back line. He will in all probability kill such lobs.

8. Pay just as much attention to your weak points as your strong ones. If possible, get some onlooker who understands the game to point out any fault he may have noticed. Practice all your weak points as much as possible. Do not mind losing practice games, but forget some of your pet strokes during practice and try and take every ball in the manner that happens to be most difficult to you.

DO'S AND DON'TS

9. Always play your best and hardest. Your motto should be 'improvement.'

10. Do not be content with thinking of the game only when you are playing it. In spare moments try and think out new strokes or methods of play, and then, when next practicing, turn your theories to practical use.

11. Play as many and as large a variety of opponents you possibly can. You will then learn to attack many kinds of defense and to defend many kinds of attack.

12. Deceive your opponents as much as possible as to the direction of your strokes. Practice looking one way and hitting the other. Practice moving your body so as to deceive your opponent as to the direction you intend placing the ball. With practice it will be found possible to move the body in almost any direction and any way, and at the same time to place the ball in any part of the court.

13. Do not play too much or too long at once. After playing for an hour or two the eye and wrist will get tired, and your play will become wanting in variety and sting. Too much play is just as bad as too little. Beware of staleness from overplay!

14. Try practicing by yourself. The service can be improved in this way. Hitting against a wall is also good practice.

15. Do not play when tired, either physically or mentally, as it is impossible to play one's best game unless fresh and on the alert.

16. Make sure of easy strokes. Do not play carelessly and do not slash wildly. The missing or 'dubbing' of an easy shot raises the morale of your opponent.

17. Variety or an all court game is the secret of success.

Change your game so as to suit every opponent. Never play the same game against two different players and if your opponent seems to be mastering you, try another method of tackling him.

CHAPTER X
PING-PONG FOR LADIES

PING-PONG for ladies is similar to that played by men, the strokes and tactics being the same. Many ladies through constant practice have become expert players and are able to give men of their own class a good battle. The margin of difference between men and women in Ping-Pong is about the same as it is in Lawn Tennis.

Their game can be improved by playing men much as our own Helen Wills Moody does. Mixed doubles, a delightful pastime by the way, will also help. The chief fault of most ladies is their tendency to make the ball bound high thus giving their opponents chances for kills.

The costume for a lady is important. She should wear an attractive sport costume with a short skirt that will permit freedom of motion. She should also have freedom of arm movement and will find low shoes most comfortable as high French heels are said to tire ankles and feet.

In conclusion, let me exhort the ladies who take up this charming and fascinating game to give it the serious attention it merits. For in the writer's opinion, there is no other game which offers so many possibilities to women to excel and play on equal terms with men. The author has been glad to learn of many ladies' tournaments held throughout the country especially in the numerous country clubs. It is a move in the right direction.

CHAPTER XI

HOW TO ORGANIZE AND RUN A PING-PONG TOURNAMENT

IN Ping-Pong, as in any other form of competitive athletics, Tournaments are the culmination of the enjoyment and the excitement stimulated by this fascinating game. To pit one's skill against the cleverness of the larger number of opponents one is able to meet in Tournaments gives a greater zest to the game. In order that the greatest enjoyment, fairest, keenest competition and finest spirit of fair play may be best assured, it is essential that all Tournaments be properly conducted with uniform authorized equipment under authoritative regulations and under the **Official Laws of Ping-Pong.**

To begin with, all Tournaments should be conducted under the jurisdiction of a committee appointed for the purpose. The chairman of this committee should be in general charge of the Tournament. The secretary of the committee should take care of all clerical details and sub-committees should be appointed as follows from the General Committee:

(a) Committee in Charge of the Equipment.
(b) Committee in Charge of the Draw.
(c) Committee on Officials.

The General Committee should not be too large nor should the sub-committees be composed of more than three members each. The General Committee naturally determines the nature of the Ping-Pong Tournament — whether it is to be inter-club, inter-team, invitation or open, for singles or doubles; the date, duration, place of play, number of entries

HOW TO RUN A PING-PONG TOURNAMENT 77

and method of securing them; the prizes, if any, to be offered; whether or not an entrance fee is to be charged and how much; and whether the Tournament is to be open to spectators or not.

EQUIPMENT. When the number of entries has been determined, the Equipment Committee, governed by the space chosen, will secure the required authorized Ping-Pong Equipment, making sure that the tables, nets, posts, rackets and balls are those adopted by **The American Ping-Pong Association** and specified in **The Official Laws of Ping-Pong.**

In considering the number of tables which can be arranged in a room of given size, it is well to bear in mind the following requirements. There should be if possible five feet between the tables as they are placed side by side and eight feet available for play at each end of a table. An excellent arrangement is to stagger the tables upon the floor, as shown in Fig. No. 1.

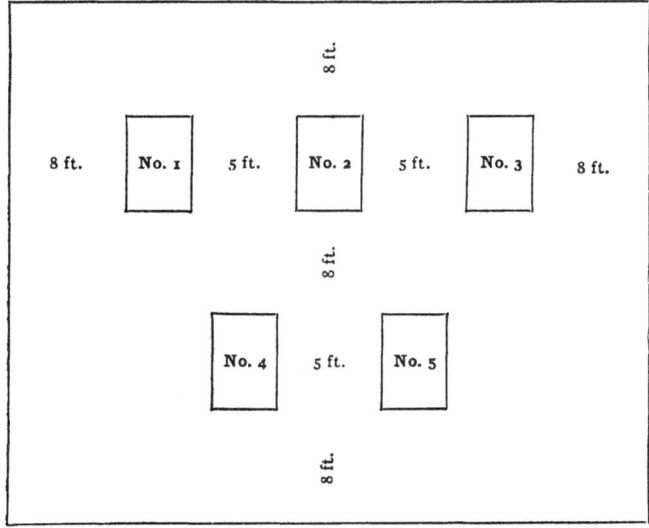

Fig. 1

In this way more space is given the players at the end of the tables and there is less probability of interference by them. After the tables have been arranged, they should be numbered consecutively. As adequate lighting facilities are important, the Equipment Committee should arrange to have at least a 100 watt lamp with a 12-inch cone shade suspended about four feet above the center of each table.

ENTRIES: The General Committee when considering the number of entries will be governed by the playing space chosen, the number of tables it can properly contain and the duration of the Tournament. To determine these factors, the number of matches that can be played upon a table in a given length of time may be estimated at 30 minutes for a two out of three game match and 45 minutes for a three out of five game match. Therefore, if a table is available for a three hour playing period, six matches — two out of three; or four matches — three out of five can be played. In these calculations, it must be remembered that in Tournament Play the preliminary matches should be two out of three games, while semi-finals and finals should be three out of five games, and that no player should be required to play more than three matches at a session, because Ping-Pong when played at its best is a strenuous game.

After the date of the Ping-Pong Tournament has been determined and the number of matches decided upon, entrance notices should be sent out by the Secretary to those who may be reasonably expected to enter. These notices should specify the place of play, the date and duration of the Tournament, the fee (if any) required, the prizes to be offered, the limit of entrance and that the Tournament shall be conducted under the authorized Official Laws of Ping-Pong

HOW TO RUN A PING–PONG TOURNAMENT 79

adopted by The American Ping-Pong Association. If the Tournament is not confined to Ping-Pong Clubs, or if not by invitation and is open to the public, then it is wise to publish this notice in a suitable newspaper.

All entries should be returnable to the Secretary before a specified date. Immediately upon receipt of the entry, the Secretary should arrange an alphabetical list giving the name and address of each entrant. This list should be delivered to the Draw Committee, which will immediately arrange the draw.

THE DRAW: In Ping-Pong there are two types of Tournaments — 'Round Robin' and 'Knockout.' In the 'Round Robin' method each player meets every other entrant. The player winning the greatest number of Matches is the Winner. In the 'Knockout' a player once defeated is out of the Tournament for good. The former method is only suitable for small informal contests, while the latter is most generally used in all Tournaments. In making the Draw, the Draw Committee should procure or prepare a Draw Sheet (see Fig. No. 2). If at all possible 8, 16, 32, 64 or 128 entrants should be secured in order to make the Draw Sheet come out

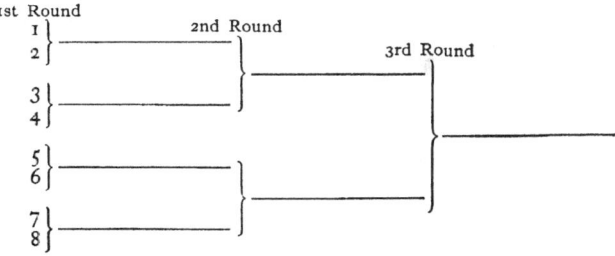

Sample draw sheet for eight players

Fig. 2

evenly. This, however, happens very infrequently. In consequence, Byes (that is blanks) are necessary and should be allotted to the first round of the Tournament. The purpose of the Byes is to bring into the second round a number of players that equals a power of 2.

BLIND DRAW. If the ability of the players is not well known the 'blind' draw shall be used. In this draw a separate slip of paper should be made for each name. These slips are drawn from a covered box and the names arranged on the draw sheet in the order in which they are drawn. As before if Byes are needed they are given to the players whose names are first drawn. Byes should be divided equally between the top and bottom of the draw sheet and should appear only in the first round. After the Draw has been completed, each player should be given a number beginning at the top of the Draw Sheet and by this number the player should be known during the Tournament.

SEEDED DRAW. If the ability of the various players is known a Seeded or selected Draw may be used in order to bring the better players together in the final rounds. If a Seeded Draw is employed, seed not less than two players and not over eight players in a Tournament consisting of 64 or less competitors. If there are more than 64 competitors, at least eight shall be seeded. For every eight entries in excess of 64, one additional may be seeded. In the sequence of their ability the seeded players should be numbered from 1 up. The No. 1 player should be placed at the top of the first half of the Draw Sheet, the No. 2 player at the top of the second half; the No. 3 player at the bottom of the first half and the No. 4 player at the bottom of the second half. Thereafter seed the players at the top of the quarters and eighths in each

HOW TO RUN A PING-PONG TOURNAMENT

half of the Draw Sheet if the Tournament is large enough. Each half of the Draw Sheet shall contain an equal number of seeded players. The names of the other entrants in the Tournament shall be written on separate slips of paper, placed in a covered box and drawn out one by one. As they are drawn, their names are placed on the Draw Sheet in order, starting from the top. If Byes are needed in the Draw, the first of these names so drawn are given the Byes and placed in the second round.

When the Draw is completed, the Committee then determines the time at which each entrant is to play his first round match. This time-schedule is then given to the Secretary whose duty it is to notify each player by a notice card reading something as follows:

MEN'S SINGLES
AMATEUR CHAMPIONSHIP TOURNAMENT
of
THE PING PONG CLUB

Branch of the American Ping Pong Association

You are Scheduled to Play Your First Round Match..Date......
at .... o'clock promptly
Place......................

On Arrival Report at once to the Secretary

All contestants not present when their match is called will be defaulted

The Public is Invited to Attend this Tournament Free of Charge

---

The Draw Committee should provide a suitable score board which shall contain names of the entrants as arranged in the draw and on this score board, the records of the matches shall be kept during the entire round. The Draw Committee should also appoint a Floor Manager, whose duty it is to assign the matches to the tables and immediately see to it that a new match is assigned to any table as soon as that table is vacated.

TOURNAMENT OFFICIALS. The Committee on Officials shall choose first a Referee who must be thoroughly familiar with the Official Laws of Ping-Pong as adopted by the American Ping-Pong Association under which the Tournament is be conducted.

The Committee shall then appoint a sufficient number of umpires so that there will always be one umpire available for each table in play. Prior to the beginning of the Tournament, the Referee shall call a meeting of the umpires and carefully instruct them in the laws, a copy of which each umpire shall have in his possession while judging the match. Each umpire will be responsible for the proper conduct of the match he is observing, and if there is objection to the ruling of an umpire by one of the contestants during the match, the ruling of the umpire shall be immediately referred to the Referee, whose decision will be final. Each umpire must be seated at the side of a table at the net post and be provided with an official score card (see page 83) on which he will make all entries as provided. Immediately a match is completed, he shall sign the score card and deliver it to the score keeper appointed by the Draw Committee who will immediately post it upon the score board. After the completion of each round of the Tournament, the Floor Manager will announce the time at which the contestants shall appear for the matches of the next round.

AMERICAN PING–PONG ASSOCIATION OFFICIAL SCORE CARD

MATCH BETWEEN

....

AND

....

1	2	3	4	5	6	7	8	9	10	11	12	13	14	15	16	17	18	19	20	21	22	23	24	25	26	27	28	29	30
1	2	3	4	5	6	7	8	9	10	11	12	13	14	15	16	17	18	19	20	21	22	23	24	25	26	27	28	29	30

1	2	3	4	5	6	7	8	9	10	11	12	13	14	15	16	17	18	19	20	21	22	23	24	25	26	27	28	29	30
1	2	3	4	5	6	7	8	9	10	11	12	13	14	15	16	17	18	19	20	21	22	23	24	25	26	27	28	29	30

1	2	3	4	5	6	7	8	9	10	11	12	13	14	15	16	17	18	19	20	21	22	23	24	25	26	27	28	29	30
1	2	3	4	5	6	7	8	9	10	11	12	13	14	15	16	17	18	19	20	21	22	23	24	25	26	27	28	29	30

1	2	3	4	5	6	7	8	9	10	11	12	13	14	15	16	17	18	19	20	21	22	23	24	25	26	27	28	29	30
1	2	3	4	5	6	7	8	9	10	11	12	13	14	15	16	17	18	19	20	21	22	23	24	25	26	27	28	29	30

1	2	3	4	5	6	7	8	9	10	11	12	13	14	15	16	17	18	19	20	21	22	23	24	25	26	27	28	29	30
1	2	3	4	5	6	7	8	9	10	11	12	13	14	15	16	17	18	19	20	21	22	23	24	25	26	27	28	29	30

..................WINNER   ....UMPIRE

In playing team matches the best method is to line up each team according to the ability of the players, the best player being No. 1, man on his team, etc. Then the No. 1 men of each team play each other, followed by the No. 2 players and so on. Five men teams will be found the most satisfactory.

THE LAWS
of
PING-PONG
Reg. U. S. Patent Office

AMENDED 1930

Copyright 1902 by Parker Brothers, Inc.
Copyright 1928 by Parker Brothers, Inc.
Copyright 1930 by Parker Brothers, Inc.

Adopted by

THE AMERICAN PING-PONG ASSOCIATION

All rights reserved

NOTICE

The word **PING-PONG** is a Registered U. S. Trademark and designates exclusively the game produced by the owners of the Trademark and Copyrights, Parker Brothers, Inc.

A. THE PING-PONG TABLE. For tournament play the table shall have a smooth, level, rectangular top playing surface, 9 feet long and 5 feet wide, stained or painted a dull, dark green with a three-quarters inch white painted line upon its outside edges and lengthwise down its center. The table may be of either the authorized folding or solid design, the top playing surface of which, when erected for play, shall be 30 inches above the floor.

For non-tournament or informal play, a folding table top 9 feet x 5 feet or 8 feet x 4 feet, marked exactly as above described, or a smaller table 8 feet x 4 feet, otherwise exactly similar to the tournament table above described, are often used, and most frequently DINING ROOM tables are utilized satisfactorily, upon which the required lengthwise center line is laid out with tape or twine, or chalk.

B. THE PING-PONG BALL. The Official ball shall be the 'Official Association Ping-Pong' ball, so branded.

C. THE PING-PONG NET AND POSTS: For tournament play the net shall be 66 inches in length, 5 inches in width with a mesh of 3/16 inch, colored green and bound with white tape. For non-tournament or informal play the net is of the same width, but the mesh may be green, yellow or white bound with white tape, the length of these nets being of the proper dimensions to suit the particular table utilized. For tournament play the authorized net is to be attached to the table top by adjustable metal extension posts. When erected the net shall be 4 feet and 6 inches from each end of the table and when adjusted for play, its top edge shall be 6¾ inches above the table's playing surface. When so attached, the net divides the table into two major courts, used for Ping-Pong Singles. The lengthwise center line divides each of the major courts into two minor courts, required for Ping-Pong Doubles.

For non-tournament or informal play, the authorized Ping-Pong metal extension posts or the authorized Ping-Pong wooden posts may be used, as is best suited to the type of table employed.

PING-PONG SINGLES

Ping-Pong Singles is the game for two players, who stand, one at each end of the table, racket in hand and strike the

THE LAWS OF PING-PONG 87

ball forward and backward over the net in conformity with the following authorized laws.

1. **THE SERVER AND THE RECEIVER:** The player who first strikes the ball across the net shall be called The Server and his opponent shall be called The Receiver.

2. **CHOICE OF SERVICE OR COURT:** The right to serve or to receive in the first game of each match shall be determined by toss. If the toss winner chooses to be Server or Receiver, his opponent shall have the choice of courts or vice versa. If the toss winner prefers, he may demand that his opponent choose first.

3. **THE MATCH, THE GAME AND THE SCORING:** The MATCH shall consist of the best two out of three games. The final match, however, in tournament play may consist of the best three out of five games, if the players so elect. THE GAME: The player first winning 21 points, wins the game, except the score be 20 all, then the player who first scores two more points than his opponent wins the game.

4. **THE CHANCE OF ENDS:** At the end of each game, the players shall interchange positions at the table ends.

5. **THE SERVICE:** Throughout a game, except at the score of 20 all, the Server shall become the Receiver and the Receiver shall become the Server after each five points. At the score of 20 all, the Server becomes the Receiver and the Receiver the Server after each point until the game is ended. The first Server in a game shall be the first Receiver in the next game of the match and so on until the match is ended.

6. **A GOOD SERVE: THE BOUNCE BALL SERVICE:** The server must stand behind his end of the table

and so strike the ball with his racket that it will bounce from the table on his (the Server's) side of the Net and passing over the Net bounce upon any portion of the table on the Receiver's side of the Net.

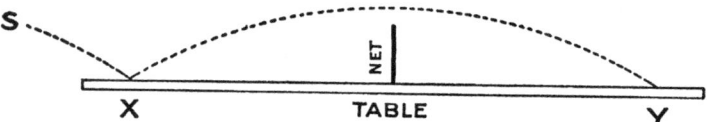

For example: S is the point at which the server's racket comes in contact with the ball. X is the point at which the ball bounces once on the server's side of the table and Y is the next point it touches.

The Server's racket and the ball must be behind the end line of the Server's court and between the imaginary extension of the table's side lines when he first strikes the ball in service. Should the Server, when serving, miss striking the ball entirely, he loses the point to his opponent.

While the above service has been adopted for Tournament play by The American Ping-Pong Association, the service previously sponsored by this association is still used in some tournaments and is optional to any branch of the American Association on previous reasonable notice to contestants. This is known as the Tennis Service, which is as follows, the minor courts (see paragraph C, page 86) are used: The service shall be delivered by the server standing behind his end of the table and projecting or dropping the ball by hand into the air. The ball shall then be struck so that it touches first within the Receiver's right minor court or the center line on his side of the net. The service is, of course, made diagonally right to left, then left to right and so alternately thereafter. Only

THE LAWS OF PING-PONG

one ball shall be served. There is no 'second or reserved service' as in Tennis.

At the moment of impact of the racket on the ball in service, both shall be behind the end line of the server's court and between an imaginary continuation of the side lines. The ball when struck, shall be below the level of the waist, and behind the end of the table, and within the limits of the width of the table. The service shall be strictly underhand; that is, when the ball is struck, no part of the racket, except the handle, shall be above the wrist. Top spin, side spin and the various other twist serves may of course be used provided the service is kept below the waist. Should the Server when serving miss the ball entirely, the stroke does not count, but should he touch the ball ever so slightly with racket or racket hand, it is a stroke and the ball is in play.

7. **A GOOD RETURN:** A player shall return the ball, correctly played onto his court by his opponent, by striking it in one stroke upon its first bounce, so that it shall pass directly over (or pass the end of) the net and touch the playing surface on his opponent's side of the table. Volleying, that is striking the ball before it bounces, is not permitted at all.

8. **THE SEQUENCE OF PLAY:** The Server having made a good serve, the Receiver shall then make a good return, and thereafter Server and Receiver shall each alternately make a good return until the point is scored.

9. **THE BALL IN PLAY:** The ball is in play from the moment at which it is tossed or dropped by hand in service until:

(a) It has touched one court twice consecutively, on the same serve or same return.

(b) It has, except in service, touched each court alternately without having been struck by the racket intermediately.

(c) It has been struck by either player more than once consecutively.

(d) It has touched either player or anything he wears, or carries, except his racket or his racket hand below the wrist.

(e) It has touched any other object except the net, supports and those above allowed.

10. **A POINT:** A point is the smallest unit of scoring. Either player shall lose the point:

(a) If he fails to make a good service.

(b) If a good service or a good return having been made by his opponent, he fail to make a good return.

(c) If he, or anything that he wears or carries, touches the net or its supports while the ball is in play.

(d) If he, or anything that he wears or carries, moves the playing surface of the table while the ball is in play.

(e) If his free hand touch the playing surface of the table while the ball is in play.

(f) If the ball, in play, comes in contact with him or anything he wears or carries before it shall have passed over the end lines or side lines and not yet having touched the playing surface on his side of the table since being struck by his opponent.

(g) If a player strike or be struck by a ball within his court before it has dropped on the table.

11. **A DEAD BALL:** A ball is dead and ceases to be in play:

(a) If a player fails to make a good service, or a good return.

(b) If the ball strikes any object, other than the net and its supports, before it drops onto the opponent's court.

THE LAWS OF PING-PONG

(c) If either player touch any part of the net or its supports with his racket or with any part of his body while the ball is in play.

(d) If the ball passes the limits of the table without dropping on the table. This is an outball and the player who stroked it out loses the point, whether or not his opponent strikes it after it has passed over the end of the table.

12. **A LET:** It is a Let and another ball must be served:

(a) If the ball served in passing over the net, touch it or its supports, provided the service be otherwise good.

(b) If a service be delivered when the Receiver is not ready, provided always that he may not be deemed to be unready if he attempt to stroke at the ball.

(c) If either player be prevented by an accident not under his control from serving a good service or making a good return.

(d) If either player lose the point owing to an accident not within his control.

13. **A FAULT:** It is a fault if the Server violates the law for serving (Rule 6). A fault by the Server is counted as one point in favor of the Receiver.

14. **A RALLY:** The period during which the ball is in play shall be termed a Rally. The scored result of a rally is termed a Point.

PING-PONG DOUBLES

The Game for Four Players

15. **PING-PONG DOUBLES** is a game for four players who play Partners in opposing pairs. The laws of play for Ping-Pong Doubles are the same as for Ping-Pong singles,

except that the table's minor courts, established by the lengthwise center line and the net (see paragraph C, page 86) are used in the Doubles service, which is necessarily changed (see Rule 17) by reason of a pair playing as partners.

16. **CHOICE OF SERVICE:** In Ping-Pong Doubles the pair who have the right to serve (see Rule 2) the first five services in any game shall decide which partner shall do so, and the opposing pair shall then decide similarly and so around until all four players have served and then the process is repeated until the game is completed.

17. **A GOOD DOUBLES SERVE:** In Ping-Pong Doubles, the service is made diagonally across the table, first right to left, then left to right and so alternately thereafter. Accordingly the Server's position must be at the right of his center line when he makes a right to left service and to the left thereof when he makes a left to right service and so shifting alternately thereafter. A good serve in Doubles is the same as a good serve in Singles (see Rule 6) except that in the first serve, the Server must so strike the ball, that after passing over the net, it bounce within the Receiver's right hand minor court or upon his center line and in the second serve it bounce within the Receiver's left hand minor court or upon his center line and thereafter the service continues so alternately.

18. **THE SEQUENCE OF DOUBLES PLAY:** The server shall make a good service, the Receiver shall then make a good return, the partner of the server shall then make a good return, the partner of the Receiver shall then make a good return, the server shall then make a good return, and thereafter each player alternately in that sequence shall make a good return.

If a player serves or receives out of turn, the mistake must

THE LAWS OF PING-PONG

be corrected as soon as discovered, unless five consecutive serves have been completed, in which event the service and receiving shall continue in the regular order and no penalty shall be imposed.

LAWN TENNIS COUNT FOR SCORING

While the 21-up method of scoring, rule 3, has been adopted by The American Ping-Pong Association for all official tournaments and matches, the Lawn Tennis Count is sometimes used for informal play.

The play is just the same as regular Ping-Pong, except that its scoring is practically the counterpart of that for out-door tennis.

In naming the score, the SERVER (for convenience) is always named first. The first point made counts a player 15, his second 15, making 30, and his third 10, making 40. His fourth point won, wins the game — (save in a deuce game).

In counting the score the word 'love' according to the custom in ancient games, is used as 'nothing.' Thus, if the SERVER, who must name his own score first, loses the first point, he would call 'Love, 15' instead of 'nothing, 15.' If the SERVER wins the next stroke, it would be 15-15, called '15 all.' If the RECEIVER wins the next point the SERVER would call '15-30' etc.

Whenever both players have 40, the score is called 'Deuce.' The next stroke won by either player is scored 'advantage' to that player. (If it is the SERVER who has the advantage, it is called 'advantage in.' If it is the RECEIVER who has advantage, it is called 'advantage out.') If the player who has 'advantage' wins the next stroke, he wins the game, but if he loses the next stroke, the score again becomes 'Deuce.' In a 'Deuce Game' the player who wins two strokes immediately following the score of 'Deuce,' wins the game.

Six Games won by either player, wins a 'SET.'

A 'Love Set' is represented by the score '6 to 0.'

A DEUCE SET is when both players have won five games. The next game won makes the score 'Advantage' to the player winning. Should the other player win the next game, the 'Set-score' returns to 'Deuce' again. The Set is WON by the player winning two games in succession immediately following the score of 'Deuce.'

AUTHORIZED EQUIPMENT

Realizing that the greatest enjoyment, the fairest, keenest competition and the finest spirit of fair play can best be insured by complete uniformity of equipment, the following standards in parts and accessories have been adopted and authorized as the best suited for the game Ping-Pong. To guarantee these essential standards of uniformity, all the authorized parts and accessories bear the mark 'Ping-Pong.'

THE PING-PONG TABLE. For tournament play the table shall have a smooth, level, rectangular top playing surface, 9 feet long and 5 feet wide, stained or painted a dull, dark green with a three-quarters inch white painted line upon its outside edges and lengthwise down its center. The table may be of either the authorized folding or solid design, the top playing surface of which, when erected for play, shall be 30 inches above the floor.

For non-tournament or informal play, a folding table top 9 feet x 5 feet or 8 feet x 4 feet, marked exactly as above

THE LAWS OF PING-PONG

described, or a smaller table 8 feet x 4 feet, otherwise exactly similar to the tournament table above described, are often used, and most frequently DINING ROOM tables are utilized satisfactorily, upon which the required lengthwise center line is laid out with tape or twine, or chalk.

THE PING-PONG BALL. The Official ball shall be the 'Official Association Ping-Pong' ball, so branded.

THE PING-PONG NET AND POSTS: For tournament play the net shall be 66 inches in length, 5 inches in width with a mesh of 3/16 inch, colored green and bound with tape. For non-tournament or informal play the net is of the same width, but the mesh may be green, yellow or white bound with white tape, the length of these nets being of the proper dimensions to suit the particular table utilized. For tournament play the authorized net is to be attached to the table top by adjustable metal extension posts. When erected the net shall be 4 feet and 6 inches from each end of the table and when adjusted for play, its top edge shall be 6¾ inches above the table's playing surface. When so attached, the net divides the table into two major courts, used for Ping-Pong Singles. The lengthwise center line divides each of the major courts into two minor courts, required for Ping-Pong Doubles.

For non-tournament or informal play, the authorized Ping-Pong metal extension posts or the authorized Ping-Pong wooden posts may be used, as is best suited to the type of table employed.

THE PING-PONG RACKET: For tournament, non-tournament or informal play, the Ping-Pong racket shall be of the dimensions illustrated in the following sketch. It may be of plain, unfinished wood, varnished wood, wood with sanded, leather, cor, or rubber blades, as suits the preference of the player.

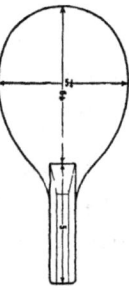

Blade, Width 5¼ inches; Length 6½ inches.
Handle, Length 5 inches

Coachwhip Publications

CoachwhipBooks.com

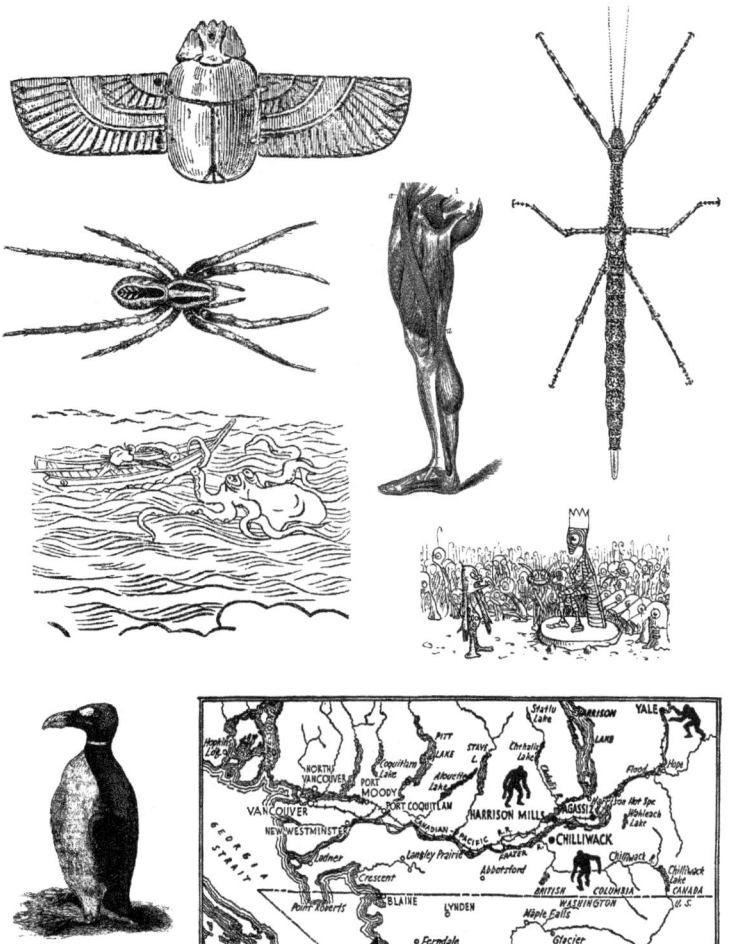

Coachwhip Publications
CoachwhipBooks.com

Complete Backgammon
ISBN 978-1-61646-134-8

Coachwhip Publications
Also Available

Pitching Horseshoes
ISBN 978-1-61646-204-8

Coachwhip Publications
coachwhipbooks.com

Croquet
ISBN 1616461446

Coachwhip Publications

Also Available

How to Hit a Golf Ball From Any Sort of Lie
ISBN 1616462035

www.ingramcontent.com/pod-product-compliance
Lightning Source LLC
Chambersburg PA
CBHW070623050426
42450CB00011B/3114